THERE ARE TWO SIDES TO EVERY COIN.

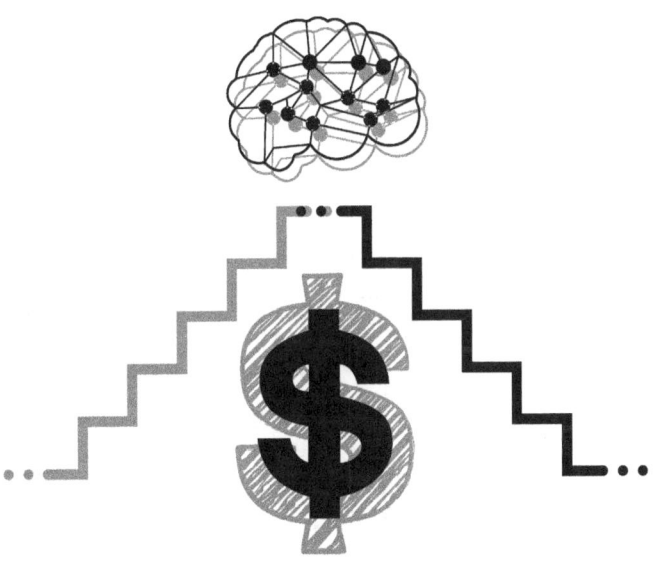

Praise for
KEVETTE MINOR KANE & TYM2THRIVE

"There are plenty of financial books on the horizon, but most of them are technical and formula driven. Here Kevette manages to combine everyday stories and lessons into processes that we can not only relate to, but also buy into. The experiences are real and relatable. Imagine two women approaching a door. As one woman enters, she holds the door for the woman who is approaching behind her. This vision perfectly depicts what you'll find in these pages. Kevette has eagerly opened the door for so many by sharing these lessons. As you maneuver through the book, you will discover many gifts and appreciate the instruction that stops in her journey have generated."

Alethia Tucker, CEO
Visionary Author & International Speaker

"Courageous and inspirational are words that I would use to describe Kevette. She has a growth mindset and uses the challenges that she has faced in her life as building blocks for her future success, with the knowledge that these experiences that she has had throughout her life have made her who she is as a person. During the writing of this book, she has reflected deeply on experiences that she has had throughout her life and how they have shaped her mindset when it comes to money management. As a therapist, I know that this self exploration can be very raw and I find Kevette to be courageous in sharing her story with us in such a personal way.

I highly recommend this book to those of you who are ready to take this journey of self exploration in mindset and money management with Kevette. She is very thoughtful in the way that she has mapped out this journey for you and she will give you many tools for you to use now and in the future. Enjoy the book and the beginning of this adventure!"

Dianne Mishra, LMSW
AWE Project Mentor

"Kevette is resilient and a game changer. We have a lot in common: we survived divorce, work hard to take care of our children, and determined to win no matter what. She is an expert in managing finances after overcoming a challenging divorce, having to start over from a lot less and she did it! I gravitate to women who have been able to achieve success after divorce as I have those that have not been able to adjust. I made a vow to Kevette that we would join forces to help others and we have through our radio shows and inspirational events for women. Being the expert that she has become, I'm sure you will be able to change your mindset about money and acquire new skills to help you with your financial goals. If anyone can do it, Kevette can!"

Tonya Barbee, MBA
Best Selling Author, Inspirational Speaker, & Coach

TYM2THRIVE
TRANSFORM YOUR MIND &
TRANSFORM YOUR MONEY
TO THRIVE

TYM2THRIVE
Transform Your Mind & Transform Your Money to Thrive

10 Steps to Self-Sufficiency

KEVETTE MINOR KANE

Financial Liberation Expert

MarimorLife LLC

MarimorLife LLC
Maryland
Copyright ©2022 by Kevette Minor Kane
Published in the United States by MarimorLife LLC

Printed in: The United States, First Edition
First Printing, 2022

Front Cover Design: Kevette Minor Kane & Sade Boyea
Cover Image: created using Canva
Interior Author Photo: Kevette Minor Kane
Back Cover Author Photo: Angela Acosta

ISBN 979-8-9863871-0-9 (paperback)
ISBN 979-8-9863871-3-0 (ebook)

For information, speaking engagements, and book signings:
MarimorLife Mindset & Money Management
Email: support@marimorlife.com
Web: www.marimorlife.com
Social: @marimorlife

This book is dedicated to every person who has ever faced a major transition in life. Also to every person who will face the transitions of life, both expected and unexpected. Remember, "Never Underestimate Your Ability to Thrive!"

This book belongs to:

_____

This book is about a message and a mission to guide people through financial education with emotional intelligence. Discussed are the five principles of Mindset Awareness and the five principles of Money Management Strategy. A literary work from author Kevette Minor Kane who is a Financial Liberation Expert based on her education and experience where surviving money trauma and financial abuse led her to thriving in both mindset and money management. Along with every chapter there is a worksheet to complete with the encouragement of progress through a positive attitude and personal productivity.

DISCLAIMER:

The contents of the book represent the personal experiences and opinions of the author. No legal responsibility or liability will be accepted for damages caused by counter-productive practices or errors of the reader. There is also no guarantee of success. The author, therefore, does not accept responsibility for lack of success, using the methods described in this book.

All information contained herein is purely for information purposes, It does not represent a recommendation or application of the methods mentioned within. This book does not purport to be complete, nor can the topicality and accuracy of the book be guaranteed. This book in no way replaces the competent personal recommendations of, or attention given by a personal financial advisor.

KEVETTE MINOR KANE

also featured in...

BOOKS

REINVENTED TO RISE:

Stories of Women Who Transformed in Order to Soar

CHAPTER 3:

From Rescue Fantasy to Full Responsibility

ORDER NOW AT

WWW.MARIMORLIFE.COM/REINVENTEDTORISE

MAGAZINES

iShine Magazine:

https://www.aandmproductions.biz/ishine-magazine

Mindset & Money Management Monthly Column

Santana Global:

https://www.santanaglobal.com/memberships

Mindset & Money Management Bimonthly Column

BLOG

MarimorLife Blog: https://www.marimorlife.com/blog

ACKNOWLEDGEMENTS

Thank you Marquel Minor,

For always being my ace. It was you and me from the beginning and I'm so proud to call you my son. Even when things haven't been the best we've learned and grown individually to continue to grow together. Love you always and forever as I continually strive to be the best mother I can be for you and your brother. Your truth is in the experience of what happened to you and in what you make happen.

Thank you Marcus Kane,

For being the best combination of two imperfect people. The best of intentions and the most love are what I have for you always. I'm so proud of you for who you've always been. My hope is for the best that life has to offer you. I do what I do to preserve generational wealth and a legacy of love for you and your brother. You two will always be my dynamic duo. Love life and live free. The truth will always be in your experience. Trust your intuition and do what's in your best interest, always.

Thank you, Mom (Cynthia Minor),

You inspired me through your example and influenced me through DNA. As a Master of Accounting and a great financial mind, you taught me through a regular routine of activity which planted a seed in my heart for Finance that continues to grow.

Thank you, Sister (Nikki Minor),

You were my first student in the pretend classroom that nurtured my love for education and has set the stage for the fulfillment of my life purpose. You are amazing.

Thank you, Diane Coy,

You treated me like a daughter and have continued to be a pillar of love and encouragement. You proofread my college application essays and you've proofread my manuscript more than 25 years later. You are the most amazing teacher and the best coach ever!

Thank you Dianne Mishra,

I'm in AWE of our connection. You are the most fabulous mentor. Your consistency and encouragement have meant the world for me getting through this process. You've comforted, motivated and celebrated me along this journey since the AWE Project brought us together. I'm so grateful for your guidance and your listening ear. You are AWE-mazing!!!

Thank you Yetsenia Munoz Suarez,

Your energy has been a constant motivation to me. Through some of the toughest times you have brightened my day with your smile and wonderful words promoting the Mary Kay way. I remember when you made me feel like a queen during one of the lowest points in my life. May your light shine forever because you are a star like no other.

Thank you Sade Boyea,

Sis, you are the D.O.P.E. Effect. Your insight has been a blessing. You speak truth and always add value. Your motivation is inspiring. Keep reaching for your goals. Make your dreams come true by continuing to be true to you, first.

Thank you Sharon Jones,

Sis, you are my hype girl forever. Your spark for life and fiery nature serve as a major encouragement to reach for the moon and dwell among the stars. You are a beacon of hope and determination. You are absolutely fabulous. Keep living life to the fullest.

Thank you Alethia Tucker,

The invitation to join the co-authors of Reinvented to Rise was exactly what I needed to begin the storytelling process. Your encouragement and confidence in me was just the support I needed to take the first step.

Thank you Tonya Barbee,

Your invitation to join the Rose Community was an amazing connection at the perfect time. Your experience is embracing. Your effort to encourage has been empowering. #iamstillarose

Thank you Candida Reid,

You saw something in me and reached out with your loving support. You challenged my perspective and encouraged me to grow. Your balanced called me to responsibility. Your loving understanding made me feel that I could forgive. You are the most amazing life coach and such a blessing to my life.

Thank you Antonio Berry,

You encouraged me to be self-sufficient. I am so grateful for all that I've learned through our friendship. Your love and support have been immeasurable.

Thank you Reginald Exum,

You reminded me very kindly from where I've come. Reaching back into the archives certainly motivated me into my own projections. And your insightful guidance helped me to find my path. I'm so grateful for every amazing reminder.

Thank you Douglas Eze,

You inspired and encouraged me to be my best and overcome the challenges that I felt were overwhelming. Your mentorship has shaped the trajectory of my career and the foundation of my financial structure. You set an example for which I'm grateful to have been exposed.

Thank you Eugene Mitchell,

For our mastermind sessions. You provided the guidance I needed and the outlet for expression that I needed to reset my mindset. You introduced me to understanding the racial wealth gap and how to close it.

Thank you Ezylfie Taylor,

For introducing me to the concept of conscious competence. You took time to guide me in the very beginning and your leadership sparked a flame.

Thank you, Troy Rawlings,

Your insight and guidance have been fundamental during this amazing transition in my life. Your counsel has been foundational and fortifying for my personal and professional development.

Thank you, James Henderson,

Inviting me to mentor the kids in your organization ignited a spark that grew into a flame for sharing financial education with our young entrepreneurs. Your work is amazing and so needed. Please continue to be a torch for their futures.

Thank you, William Holmes,

For the networking invitations and your sage advice about my reestablishment. You reminded me of who I had been and encouraged me to reach for who I could be. Your success has been a motivation and an inspiration.

Thank you, Scott Gregory,

For inviting me to cohost Money Mindset Mondays with you on Clubhouse. For more than a year this platform has provided an opportunity for us to share knowledge and insight through the conversations that have triggered personal and professional growth. Seeing your journey as an author and coach has been inspiring and confirming.

CONTENTS

Dedication   ix
Acknowledgements   xiii
Foreword   xxiii
Preface   xxv

INTRODUCTION

I. Emotional Intelligence   5

II. Financial Education   7

III. Self-Sufficiency   10

SIDE 1: MINDSET

Mental Awareness   23

#MINDFULMONEYMOMENT: My Money Talk   27

Emotional Awareness   28

#MINDFULMONEYMOMENT: My Financial Feelings   34

Three Spiritual Awareness 35

#MINDFULMONEYMOMENT: My Money Vibe 44

Four Physical Awareness 45

#MINDFULMONEYMOMENT: My Health is Wealth 50

Five Financial Awareness 51

#MINDFULMONEYMOMENT: My Financial Routine 56

MINDSET RESET

SIDE 2: MONEY MANAGEMENT

Six Cashflow 64

#MINDFULMONEYMOMENT: My Abundance Flow 72

Seven Credit Strategy 73

#MINDFULMONEYMOMENT: My Credibility 77

Eight Savings Strategy 78

#MINDFULMONEYMOMENT: Saving for My Life 82

Nine Investment Strategy 83

#MINDFULMONEYMOMENT: My Best Interest   88

Insurance Strategy   89

#MINDFULMONEYMOMENT: My Life & Legacy   94

TRANSITION

About The Author   100

FOREWORD

In Greek mythology, the phoenix is a bird that is a symbol of renewal and rebirth. It is reputed to bring good luck, harmony, peace, balance, and prosperity. Its outstanding characteristic is that near the end of its life cycle, it builds and retreats to a nest that it ignites. The bird is consumed by the flames but, from its ashes, another phoenix arises, and the cycle begins anew.

I have known Kevette Minor Kane since her days as a bright, talented, beautiful student and cheerleader at the high school where I taught. Although teachers and coaches are warned against having favorites, Kevette was always secretly one of mine. Triumphing over monetary constraints and a sometimes-challenging home life, Kevette earned a scholarship to Morgan State University in Baltimore and graduated with a Bachelor of Science degree in finance.

As her life progressed, Kevette rose up and escaped from a suffocating marriage and a life of poverty in a foreign country to return to the United States and begin a new life cycle as a successful financial expert. Her mission: to share her life's journey and assist other women in their journey to become financially stable and independent.

The Kevette Minor Kane that I know, just like the legendary phoenix, has been able time and time again to rise from the ashes of misfortune, using her strength and intelligence, to create a better life for herself and those who seek her advice.

For any woman looking for guidance in navigating the often rough and confusing waters of financial empowerment and security, I cannot imagine a better guide than Kevette Minor Kane and her book, TYM2THRIVE.

Diane Coy
Educator, Administrator, & Coach

PREFACE

Every person has a purpose. The challenge is to discover that purpose and the joy is in its fulfillment. My purpose is to share and encourage this message with regard to "transforming your mind and transforming your money to thrive." I've had some tough experiences that were the result of some very poor choices. I've learned some valuable lessons that I'm able to turn into blessings by sharing them with you. This book serves as a baseline of awareness and the fundamental strategies for you to build upon as you progress on your journey to self-sufficiency. It's all about Mindset & Money Management. It has been created to serve as a guide by teaching you to understand how your emotions affect your money management and how your feelings affect your financial decisions. From the surface to the root, it's about being able to make better decisions, create better habits and experience a greater quality of life. I'm here to encourage you to take back your financial power, increase your confidence during uncertain times, and be intentional as you find and fulfill your purpose in life.

In May of 2020, I began this project as part of my healing process. I've always been a writer and I've written several books in the past that never came to the point of publishing because I chose to listen to the discouraging words of those in my closest circle of influence. So, when I made a commitment and invested in the process of writing this book, it was a big deal for me. Since then, this project has shifted and grown and shifted again. I ran into more challenges and decided to take a pause and then the Universe gave me the encouragement I needed. When Alethia Tucker reached out to invite me to participate in her visionary project, an anthology that changed my life, I was ready, and it was the perfect segue. The title alone touched my heart and brought me to tears, "Reinvented to Rise: Stories of Women Who Transformed in Order to Soar." When I read the invitation message, I knew right away that this was the universe extending me an olive branch. It was finally time for me to share my story.

This has truly been a healing journey for me. Not exactly as I had imagined or planned. However, certainly every step that I needed to make the healthy progress required for me to establish a firm foundation for educating, guiding and supporting every person who might benefit through this process. For so many years up until that point I stood strong under the weight of having been told over and over again that no one wanted to hear what I had to say. Either by word or deed those in my closest circle of influence had often condescended my ideas and discouraged any option that might have presented an opportunity for me to share them. Now however, as a co-author I had an opportunity to work with an amazing group of ladies who were just the encouragement that I needed. They were my team and they made me feel that I was not alone in this process. So, I was able to introduce myself as a published writer and share my story of transition which led to my transformation without feeling like a spotlight with the heat of exposure was beaming down on me.

The chapter I wrote in that book was pivotal in its purpose and in the writing. I chose the title of my chapter to reflect the process and the lesson I learned in a summary of what I had experienced during my recovery. I called it, "From Rescue Fantasy to Full Responsibility. I spoke of how I survived multiple traumas in order to transform my life and flip the switch into thrive mode. You can get a copy of that book from my website at www.marimorlife.com/reinventedtorise. Purchasing a copy from me directly will also ensure that I receive the financial reward for all my efforts both in creating and promoting that work. I thank you in advance for your encouragement and support.

When this journey began for me, I was but a smoldering ember. Several experiences, which I'll describe in the biographical part of this series, contributed to sparking the flame that now burns within me. My hope here is that you will be ignited and allow your flame to flourish from within. My first encouragement is to simply breathe. (See the MarimorLife Mindset Reset Exercise) A flame needs oxygen to survive so when you take a deep breath know that you are feeding the fire within you that will serve as a light to the world. It is by sharing your lessons that they too will become blessings. Education is the method of elevation that eliminates any option except your ultimate success.

I educate through seminars, workshops and courses, either virtual or in-person. I guide by providing financial planning, business strategy and mindset coaching services. I support through the MarimorLife Community established for

Mindset & Money Management to encourage and empower every member toward financial literacy and self-sufficiency. I am both educated and experienced where financial management is concerned. I do this work for others because I've done this work for myself first. I recognize some of the advantages I've had through education and situations that have allowed me an insight that can benefit those willing to hear my story and apply the tips and strategies I've found to be successful.

My mission is to elevate women worldwide to a greater quality of life. As an educator, a public speaker, and an author, I share my message of financial liberation through a transformational process which incorporates emotional-mental well-being with improved financial habits for continued success. In this book I will reveal that transformational process. I hope that you will find the basics of this process for consideration and application. I also hope that you may find confidence and satisfaction in accomplishing your own goals. It's about knowing what to do and understanding how to do it. As you take action to complete the tasks that can contribute to a healthy routine, then you will create the strategy that leads you to success.

Never Underestimate
Your Ability to
Thrive!

INTRODUCTION

Many people have had to start over in life financially because of various circumstances out of their control, traumatic situations, or even poor decisions. Many have had to start from rock bottom knowing that the only option was to go up from that point. But what if you have to start from the dust. When you've been what I call "under broke," the hole you have to get out of feels like a pit blasted through rock bottom. The big question then, is how do you rebuild from that place? Well, it's been said that dust mixed with tears makes clay, so then you can make bricks and begin to rebuild.

The hardest part about anyone taking a deep look into their finances is feeling like what they have is not enough. Understanding where that feeling comes from requires a look back in time to your introduction to money. The first memories you have about money are based on the influence of those essential people in your life. Their interactions and expressions made an impact on you at the very earliest stages of life, before you could even walk and talk. This is even having an effect on your relationship with money right now. Are you clear about how much money you actually have? Do you know exactly how much money you're going to need, in the next week, month, or year?

Many people don't have any idea what these numbers are, or even how to consider them. Calculating these numbers can be an overwhelming task that is adamantly avoided until it's an absolute requirement. If this sounds like your experience, or that of someone close to you, then you've come to the right resource to support you in improving the situation.

So, how do you know what is the right direction? And how do you keep moving forward? Well, let's start by examining both sides of the coin. On the one side you have *mindset* and on the other side you have *money management.* The key though is to understand the correlation between the two. When you understand how your mindset affects your money management, then you can create a plan including the tasks necessary for you to accomplish in order to achieve your goals and thrive in life. I believe that a financial plan is as individual to a person as their fingerprints. However, I encourage you to also recognize at various stages in life your financial plan will need to be updated according to the changes of life.

In this book we will review the five principles of *mindset awareness* including: mental, emotional, spiritual, physical and financial, and the five strategies of money management including: cashflow, credit, savings, investment, and insurance, so as to better understand the full scope of your finances. As you become more conscious of influences from your past, you will understand how you got to where you are presently. The hard part can be recognizing and taking responsibility for the role you've played in getting yourself to where you are currently. There will be many situations and circumstances that were completely out of your control so, you may ask, why would you take responsibility for what was not in your control? Well, it's not the uncontrollable events but rather your responses to those events that must be owned. "Stuff" happens to everyone, right? What makes the difference in the outcome is how you respond to or handle the "stuff". That's your part.

Once you've identified how the your responses have contributed to an effect then you will also recognize that you hold that same power right now. With that responsibility accepted then you will be able to also take responsibility as you set new goals and identify the tasks necessary to accomplish them. When you understand how your decisions, habits and experiences from the past have contributed to where you are in the present, then you will be able to make better decisions, create better habits and experience a greater quality of life moving forward.

Understanding how our emotions affect our financial decisions allows us to take back our financial power by managing our money so that we can experience the self-sufficiency necessary to fulfill our purpose in life. We must each recognize for ourselves that there is no way we can arrive at that level of empowerment unless we first explore where we lost our power and why we may be continuing to give it away. It is only when we transform our mindset that we are able to transform our money management and recognize that we possess the ability to thrive. There is a critical equation here: **Emotional Intelligence + Financial Education = Self-Sufficiency**

So, let's talk about what this means and how it can influence your mindset and money management.

I. Emotional Intelligence

IDENTIFY - COPE - SHIFT

Emotional intelligence is more about emotional awareness than emotional control. However, emotional control, along with healthy emotional expression, is the goal of becoming more emotionally intelligent. Having the ability to manage interpersonal relationships empathetically and judiciously is absolutely critical, and it all begins with being conscious of how you feel.

In this book we will evaluate how you feel when you think about, talk about or make decisions about money. First, however, we must acknowledge one basic truth. Every decision we make where money is involved is either triggered by emotion or triggers an emotional response. How you feel about money goes back beyond what you can consciously remember in childhood. At the earliest stages of life in your development you were influenced by those you first saw handling, interacting around, and even speaking about money. What's amazing is that we are affected by those early experiences even in our present day lives. What's more important is how we are affected and how this influence will carry out into our future lives.

Have you ever had someone tell you that "money doesn't grow on trees"? How about the saying that "money burns a hole in your pocket"? Beliefs like these have a major impact on the way we treat our money, and the way money makes us feel. There are emotions on both sides of this relationship. You save or spend money based on your emotions, and you have an emotional response when you save or spend money. It's not a question. That's simply a fact. It's how you manage those emotions and the decisions you make as a result that really makes the difference in your life and the outcome of the situation.

Have you ever thought that rich people were mean and greedy because of their money? As a result have you decided never to be that way? Where did you get that idea? A person's relationship with or emotional response to money can be determined by or connected to the first memories they have in which someone close to them interacted with money. Those first memories can shape a person's relationship with money from childhood into adulthood. So, my question is, what is your first money memory? Who was your first money influencer? Do the answers to these questions present a challenge? Has the influence you've been under put you in a place where you feel financially unsatisfied? If so, then know that you will benefit from the financial education, guidance, and support that will come as you complete the reading of this book along with the outlined exercises and worksheets to take the next steps on your journey to self-sufficiency. In redefining your goals and taking the actions necessary to accomplish them, you have the ability to thrive. You've found yourself in the right place. So, be sure to connect with MarimorLife Mindset & Money Management online by joining the MarimorLife Community at www.marimorlife.com and connect across social media: @marimorlife.

So how do you change your relationship with money if your influence from the very beginning has presented a challenge? That's just one of the questions this book will answer for you.

II. Financial Education

LEARN - DO - TEACH

Financial Literacy is having the knowledge, skill and ability to make effective financial decisions. Financial Education is how you get there. When you learn and understand how money works, then you can make better decisions about how to make it work for you. Getting to know about financial systems and what's in your best interest are only the start, but certainly the foundation you will need to build a financial plan and portfolio that meets your personal preferences. I like to refer to this process as building your financial house. Being guided through this process by a professional advisor, like myself, will ensure that your financial house is up to code and will stand as an asset for generations to come.

Start where you are building your foundation with what you have right now. A literal foundation must be dug out and leveled to prevent any future instabilities that could cause a crack in the foundation and render the home unlivable. The same thing applies with your financial foundation. We start by digging into the ground to level it out. In financial terms, that means organizing your budget by understanding your income and expenses to know where to manage your cash flow. There are only two things you can ever do with money. That is to save it or to spend it. The order in which you do those two things will determine the outcome of both your lifestyle and your legacy as you build wealth or create debt. You get to decide, and you must understand that there's more involved than just creating a simple budget.

I encourage every person to embrace financial education so that they can identify their goals and create an action plan to organize their financial life. When we work together, we are able to take back your financial power to fulfill your purpose in life and demonstrate your ability to thrive. Start where you are and be willing to do the work. That's only the first step on this journey. Taking your next step is absolutely critical to actually reaching your goal. So, keep putting one foot in front of the other and keep a perspective of growth.

The next level is to take what you've learned and share it with someone else. Financial education is more than just being able to add a few numbers and record a simple budget. That, of course, is the start. However, being financially educated means understanding how to balance a budget and knowing the principles that lead to effective money management. Financial Literacy on the other hand means being able to manage your money so that its value increase and your bottom line stays in the black.

#TYM2THRIVE TIP: Black is the color used to describe a positive financial balance while red is the color used to describe or identify a negative financial balance.

Demonstrating financial literacy versus gaining financial education can be compared to reading literacy and reading education (learning how to read). When we speak about being literate its because you are able to demonstrate the skill by reading a piece of literature. Some might add that literacy includes comprehension. Understanding of what you've read is a critical piece of this literacy puzzle. Same thing with financial literacy. This involves not only reading a financial report but understanding its significance. Also, demonstrating your ability to make decisions in your financial best interest.

III. Self-Sufficiency

FREEDOM - INDEPENDENCE - LIBERATION

There are a few key words used to describe a positive financial position in life.

- **Financial freedom** is the term used to describe a person who is free of constraint such as that which comes with owing a debt. Thus, they are not a "slave to the lender".
- **Financial independence** is the term used to describe when a person is not subject to the control of others for money. A great example is when a person is not looking to an employer for a paycheck.
- **Financial liberation** is freedom from traditional financial roles and attitudes. That perspective will be discussed throughout this publication.

At different stages in your financial life, you may be able to claim financial freedom or independence. However, my encouragement comes more from the perspective of understanding and encompassing liberation, which is the goal of this mindset and money management transformation. It's about understanding that there is a balance between the independence of "I don't need anyone because I can decide and do everything by myself," (trauma response) and the codependence of "I can't move without the permission of another person validating my decision and the action that follows," (the effects of financial abuse). When we recognize the reality of our interdependency in life then we are better able to manage our financial decisions to create good financial habits that lead to wealth creation and maintenance. It's time to let go of that old scarcity mindset and get liberated.

I want you to know from this day forward that everything you already have is absolutely enough. Enough to get started, enough to build momentum, enough to accomplish your dreams, when you decide to take the next step and keep moving forward. I am here to assist you with that process by sharing my expertise in financial liberation to reveal your ability to thrive.

SIDE 1: MINDSET

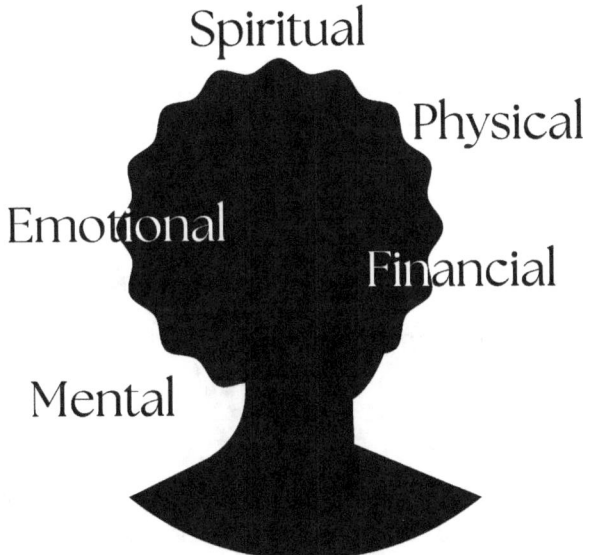

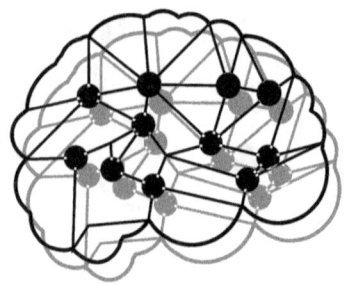

*Perspective is like an angle in photography,
a slight shift can give you a completely different
point of view.*

The key to a strong Mindset is an elevated conscious-ness. Awareness of yourself, awareness of your environment, awareness of shifting situations and changing circumstances and how all these factors affect you. If you are truly aware of yourself and your environment, then you may be able to manage the situations and circumstances that come up both expectedly and unexpectedly in a more beneficial way. However, a lack of awareness may leave you wondering and questioning without the confidence to make good decisions in order to create a more beneficial outcome. For example, if you are driving on the road and you are aware of the cars around you. When someone makes a move that could put you in danger, in your awareness, you are able to respond in a way that may prevent an accident or at least minimize the damages. However, when an unexpected move is made and an accident occurs, a lack of awareness increases the chance of maximum impact and the damages that result may be irreparable.

Thinking ahead also allows you to minimize the loss due to preparation by way of various insurances for protection, from a financial perspective. When you are unconscious or unaware of certain possibilities then you may not take the necessary steps for prevention or protection and that will end up costing you more in the end.

When money challenges your mindset, Money Trauma and Financial Abuse may be the hurdles to overcome with regard to money management. Money Trauma is when someone has experienced financial limitation that has affected their course of life either predictably or unexpectedly, at times unpreventable and often resulting in the development of a Post-Traumatic Stress Disorder, in this case, known as Financial PTSD. Financial Abuse, on the other hand, is when a person's finances are purposefully manipulated or withheld creating financial distress as the result of a perpetrator seeking to limit the current or future access to financial resources resulting in disruption of access to life essentials for the one being abused.

While Money Trauma may be the result of either poor decisions or unforeseen occurrences out of the control of the one suffering the trauma, financial abuse is intentional and targeted. Money Trauma can be a solitary experience. However, Financial Abuse always involves more than one person or entity; one as the abuser and one as the subject of abuse. The greatest challenge for most people is recognizing that the trauma or abuse even exists or has been experienced. Oftentimes people, both women and men, are taught simply to ignore their pain and push through to progress forward. What often goes unaddressed is the residual effect from improperly healed or unhealed mindset injuries that are the result of this trauma and abuse.

The unhealed emotional wounds may also trigger what's known as a trauma response which occurs similar to a deja vu experience. Let me explain. It's been identified that what's actually happening when a person experiences deja vu is that the brain is pulling together small bits of familiar information from many past experiences to make us feel as though we are reliving the exact same situation or scenario as once before. While we are not able to consciously recall the specific past experience (because it may not even exist) our brain makes all the connections for us based on triggers in our sensory memory, including sight, smell, sound, taste or touch. When a trauma response occurs, another major sense is triggered called our somatic nervous system. This causes a response in our somatic memory. You see, our brain remembers everything.

So, when we have a traumatic experience there is a physical response or reaction that occurs. It may be that our muscles get tense, our breath gets short, we start to sweat, etc. This happens because the hormones in our body have been triggered for us to respond with what's often been called the "fight or flight response". Our somatic nervous system is what controls those voluntary muscular actions in order for us to protect ourselves. So, just like with deja vu, when we experience a trauma response the situation or scenario triggers the recognition of familiarity in our brain, only in this case it's not those happy memories that are so dearly cherished. It's more likely a situation in which you had to defend yourself or escape in order to protect yourself. Understand that the situation doesn't have to be exactly the same for the triggers to occur.

To describe the reaction that is a trauma response I'll refer to a ball rolling off a table. If you've ever seen that happen before then you know that once the ball rolls off the table, it will hit the floor if there's nothing to interrupt the fall. What a person might do when they see the ball roll off is reach out to catch it. This is a voluntary muscular response although in a familiar situation the reaction happens so quickly that it may appear to be involuntary. There is a similar effect with the emotional response to a traumatic event. When there are enough environmental cues that trigger the brain's sense of familiarity then the emotional response to those triggers would seem involuntary. However, knowing that the action is controlled by the somatic nervous system which supports voluntary muscular reactions can support a person in raising their level of consciousness to understanding the amount of control they truly have over the reaction they express.

An initial trauma response may occur with a certain unconscious reaction (although voluntary) so the way a person gains control over the trauma response is to become conscious of the triggers and their somatic memory in order to shift the behavior and determine a different, hopefully healthier, response. This healing is the process of becoming emotionally intelligent. (Read Emotional Intelligence)

To overcome the challenges, you must pay attention to the details of how you learn in addition to what you learn. That is what we call the process of conscious competence. Conscious competence is empowering because when you recognize the steps you yourself have taken to gain knowledge and insight then you will be able to comprehend the underlying motivation and the details of the process. This is especially helpful when you have the goal of sharing with another person what you have learned. When you can recall what you did, then you become a great teacher. When you can recall how you did it, then you become a great mentor. This sharing of wisdom can be more valuable than learning through direct experience because of the time and opportunity for loss spared the one being advised. You have two choices; pay attention to learn, prepare and prevent OR pay for your lack of knowledge, wisdom and insight with the first-hand experience that will provide a valuable lesson because of what it cost you in time, energy, and money.

This process of being conscious or paying attention is the very foundation of mindset as it affects your thinking, your feelings, your connection, your physical experience and your finances. Understanding the five main principles of Mindset Awareness contributes to a wholistic perspective which contributes to the confidence that comes with being complete. These awarenesses include: the mental, the emotional, the spiritual, the physical and the financial. Like having all the pieces to the puzzle. Even if you haven't completed the puzzle, knowing that all the pieces are there gives you a level of confidence as you move forward to complete the big picture. The same confidence can exist for you in life when you have all the pieces to your own big picture. There is time and effort required to understand your own mindset and to remain conscious, however the benefits far out way the costs when considering the experience of driving. You see, a conscious driver will make sure to take both preventative and protective measures by maintaining their vehicle and protecting it properly. On the other hand, a driver who is unconscious or unaware may not care for proper maintenance which could cause an accident that then costs them time, damages to the vehicle and injury to a person with no measures to recoup financial or material losses. This leaves them in an unbeneficial position as a result of their poor thinking and lack of competence.

Mindset is where Money Management begins. However, the process of managing your money well may be challenged when trauma and/or abuse become factors in the scenario. The same way the principles of mindset have been identified, so may the types of traumas exist because trauma has a direct effect on your mindset. Trauma is the emotional response to a shocking event that leaves a person with unpredictable symptoms or side-effects including but not limited to emotional overwhelm, a sense of denial, and even some discomforting physical reactions such as dizziness, nausea, or headache.

Identifying a traumatic event is based upon the interpretation of the one having the experience. It is my belief that every person living has experienced trauma to some degree. The challenge is when it comes to recognizing the trauma and managing the response. From your mind to your heart, out of your mouth and into your environment, you will act accordingly with your money. You create your own reality. What can you imagine? What will you manifest?

I understand financial trauma because I've been there. During a period of less than two years I experienced three major traumatic events including: surviving Hurricane Maria in Puerto Rico on September 20, 2017, losing my father in death on December 7, 2018, and the dissolving of my marriage on April 24, 2019. These are not the only traumatic events that I've experienced as you'll read when you get to the "life lessons" part of this series. However, I recognize how every traumatic experience has had an effect on my mindset and I've been able to create an effective reset technique as a result of "doing the work".

What did I do during those trying times? I got quiet, I prayed and meditated, then I spoke about my experiences and wrote in my journals pouring out all of my emotions. I searched for the lessons in order to recognize the blessings. I often experienced episodes of traumatic response. I fell to my knees so that I could heal and there were days when laying down was my only option, but I absolutely refused to give up on myself and the life I knew my Source, the Creator, had intended for me. You see, the life I had planned for myself no longer existed, but a new life has been given to me and that's why I am sharing this with you today.

It's about understanding the past to make present connections with a focus on accomplishing future goals. This is about understanding the opportunity that today provides for each and every one of us. If we compare life to a garden, then we must have fertile soil and a new seed to plant. That new seed can sprout when nurtured and cultivated with care. You are that seed, and this is the care that you need.

So when I sit down with my clients and they share the story of what has happened to them with me, I do not take a position of judgment, because I've been there. And that's why I can not only show you WHAT to do for yourself, but I can also show you HOW to accomplish your goals, because I've done the work for myself first. Today I am living self-sufficiently, and I know that you can too.

I am proud of what I have been able to accomplish, and you will be proud when you look back on this day and see how far you've gone and how much you've been able to accomplish. So, let's make a pledge for Financial Liberation in your life.

When I started out, I had nothing. I had no home, no transportation, no job, no bank account, only hope and determination. Awesome thing is that's all the Universe needs from any of us. Who knew that in less than two years I would be able to establish a firm financial foundation and grow to support others in doing the same things for themselves?

I started by finding work to establish a steady income and keeping my expenses to a minimum. I set up my cashflow accounts to track my spending and started a business to increase my income. Then I focused on turning around my credit by raising my score over 200 points in less than six months. I began contributing to my savings plan for the future by establishing a retirement account for myself. I've made a few small investments that have already yielded dividends and will continue to grow over the long term. And finally, I set up my first independent life insurance policy to begin creating a legacy of wealth for my children. And there is more to come.

This may seem like a lot to some and not very much to others. What matters most though isn't what I've done for myself but rather what you have an opportunity to do for you and *your future self*. When you have nothing, getting started seems like the most challenging thing in the world. However, taking that first step is like taking a giant leap to the moon. Once you've been there you know that you can go farther. So, let's go.

| one |

Mental Awareness

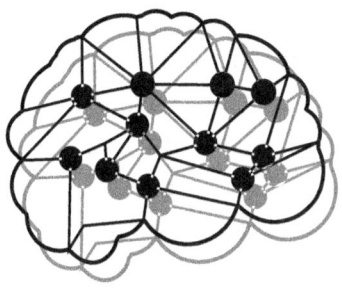

Pay Attention to Your Thoughts

From your mind to your heart, out of your mouth, into your environment and through your finances, mental awareness is where everything starts. There is a saying that goes "money talks and BS walks." If you've ever heard it before then the intended explicative for "BS" probably came to mind.

However, I'd like to challenge that thought by substituting the words "Belief System". So now the saying is "Money Talks and Belief Systems Walk". Do you get that?

Contrary to what many believe, money is not innately bad or inherently evil. Money is simply an actuator or an activator in any scenario, thus "money talks" by granting the opportunity for an action to be taken. However, it is the person's belief system that perpetuates their actions based on the availability, or the lack, of money. So, essentially, money doesn't make people do good or bad things. Rather, people do good or bad things with money based on their belief systems.

So the real question comes down to how they have established their belief system. To answer this question for yourself, you would need to evaluate your influences, education and experiences with regard to money. Your *money memory* which is the basis of your *money story* is the basis of your current *money beliefs*. Your experiences up to this point, including any traumas you have endured, have shaped your present *money relationship*. You, however, have the power to shift the *story* and *beliefs* to improve the *relationship* once you understand the *memories*. Everything that's ever happened to you serves a purpose when you learn the lessons and turn them into blessings for yourself and others. How you identify those blessings is determined by your acceptance and application of the lesson for your best interest. Your thoughts are where everything begins. Your thoughts are like the first domino in an elaborate scheme because everything else falls into place based upon your mentality. This also works in the reverse such that how things fall into place in your life will have an effect on your mentality. Being conscious of these causes and effects gives you the power to determine your response and thus the impact of the outcome.

To this end I recommend the removal of two words from your vocabulary; try and can't. It's not about your inability but rather about your refusal to allow less than what you desire or deserve. Operating from a place of fear creates a sense of scarcity and produces the reality of lack. When you make the statement that you're going to try something you confirm that you're going to make an effort, but your expectation is not to succeed. If your expectation is not to succeed, then there's only one other option available for the outcome and that is failure. So essentially you're setting the expectation of failure. On the other hand, if you speak about something as you're going to do it, then you set the expectation of success. Regardless of how many attempts are made you have set the expectation of not settling for failure because you have limited yourself to the only option of accomplishing your goal. The other option would be that you set the expectation of not doing because you've decided not to make any attempt. This is not the same as if you'd tried and failed because you made a clear choice and that is empowering. How you speak, determines the energy put forth and absolutely has a real effect on the outcome.

This outcome is less about where you actually are in life but rather is more about where you believe you can be in life. You may wonder why some people start off life in the poorest of conditions and end up living richly or why some people start off life in the richest of conditions and end up living poorly. The simple answer is that it's all a state of mind.

Henry Ford said it best, "whether you think you can or you think you can't, you're right."

What we must understand is that what our mind can imagine is what we are able to create in our reality. The good part is the manifestation of our dreams while the hard part is the manifestation of our traumas. Now, pause for a moment and take a deep breath, because what I'm not saying is that anyone is to blame for the bad things that happen to them. What I am saying though is that until we take responsibility for the fact that we can shift our reality by changing our thoughts then we may always exist as a victim of circumstances. What I want to encourage you is that you can triumph over every negative circumstance or situation by choosing to have a positive perspective, being productive and tracking your progress.

Mental Awareness is the measure of consciousness that comes with self-examination and introspection beyond the surface of specific situations and circumstances. It's more like digging to the root of your experiences to understand if there's a need for pruning versus excavation (i.e., the garden).

Now let's take an opportunity to review and possibly reveal your money memory.

#MINDFULMONEYMOMENT:
My Money Talk

What do I personally believe about money?

_____

_____

_____

_____

_____

What money trauma and/or financial abuse have I experienced?

_____

_____

_____

_____

_____

| two |

Emotional Awareness

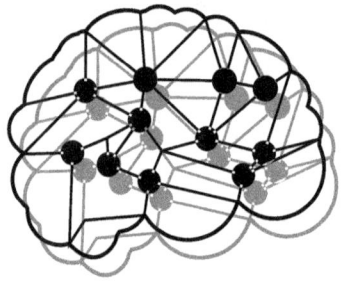

PAY ATTENTION TO YOUR FEELINGS

When you open your eyes in the morning there is a sense that comes about you, a feeling that sets the tone of your day as you wake up after having rested. Emotional awareness is the consciousness concerning how you feel. It's about understanding the thoughts that trigger your feelings. Are you emotionally aware? Are you really aware of your emotions? Do you take a moment to process how you feel and why you feel that way? Do you understand how to shift your mood by addressing your thoughts and the mental narrative you have created for yourself?

Every day you wake up with a new opportunity to feel better and to be better. When you are emotionally aware you will take the time to do the work that gets you there. Having a morning routine, I believe is one of the most stabilizing and fortifying habits to create. Your motivation to take the actions necessary to accomplish your goals will determine how far you get on the journey to creating the life of your dreams. There are a few factors that contribute to our feelings, however, each of them is directly connected to our thoughts because our thoughts are the connection between our brain and our heart. Whether it's memories from the past or a present situation or a future anticipation, what we think dictates how we feel.

All five principles of mindset awareness are interconnected. While I've taken the perspective of identifying and explaining them each separately in this book for the purpose of clarity, you may notice an overlap as you read along. With that point noted I bring your attention to the fact that our physical senses trigger our emotional responses. What we see, hear, smell, taste and touch, causes a direct emotional reaction based on our personal perspective and preferences. Our environment contributes to our happiness, our sadness, our joy and our fears. All of these emotions we have the power to control within ourselves, yet they may be significantly influenced by outside factors that we may have no control over.

When you think about the notion of why you want what you want, a lifetime of influences must come into consideration. This means understanding how your environmental exposure and the influence of key people in your life contributes to your belief system and the responses that result in various situations and circumstances. The tough part is examining yourself through a lens of introspection when your desire is to shift a behavior or change a narrative to improve your experience of life moving forward.

In many cases, people have been taught not to think much of themselves. Especially those coming from middle class and low-income backgrounds. These individuals are often told to consider the welfare of others above their own believing that regardless of their choice to suffer, that eventually they will have their needs met through some mysterious act or that they should develop the strength to endure without having their own needs met. I want to challenge that thought process right now by asking you to consider that while we humans are resilient and capable of sacrifice and survival even under the most drastic and traumatic conditions, our life was not intended for an eternal state of suffering for the benefit of others. When you give to someone else out of your need, you only end up needy or destitute. You may have helped another person, however giving in such a way will prove to be more detrimental than good.

When you sacrifice yourself to give to someone else it's like pouring out from a half full cup. Yes, the cup is half full and that identification shows that you have a positive perspective (because you didn't identify the cup as being half empty). However, any amount that you give from your half full cup only means that your cup will now be less than half full. If you keep giving from that depleted cup it will eventually be empty. So while you've contributed to the well-being of those around you, hurting yourself in the process made the entire effort a negative experience. This poor thinking will lend you consistently to a position of not having enough to care for yourself.

If, on the other hand, you find a way to ensure that your cup is full consistently and only determine to give to others from your overflow or extra, then you will never allow the depletion of your personal resources. This level of maintenance is beneficial for both yourself and others because they will see your example and may be motivated to fill their own cup. At the very least, having clear boundaries about giving only from your overflow will set a clear standard for your quality of life.

A healthier perspective is to focus on the relationship you have with yourself first. Having a full cup is equivalent to putting your mask on first in an airplane when the cabin pressure changes. If you deplete your cup and end up with nothing left for yourself, then you're no good to anyone else. So, ensuring that you keep a full cup means also having the ability to serve others from a healthy place. This is where you demonstrate understanding the balance between being selfish, caring for yourself without concern for others, with being selfless, caring for others without concern for yourself. The balance is what I call having a self-first attitude such that you care for yourself first. In that way you may be able to serve others from your overflow in abundance. I call this your abundance-flow.

Pay close attention to the words you think and speak about money. Imagine that money is an invisible friend sitting in on every conversation hearing what you say about her. If she becomes offended by your words or tone, she may simply choose not to be around. Be careful to speak positively even when she's not fully present. It's funny how a person can feel the negative energy that exists when someone has been speaking poorly of them. Sometimes we aren't able to pinpoint the source, yet we pick up that uneasy feeling and may just decide not to hang around.

Money behaves in the same way. Being a currency, there is an energy and vibration that is inherent with money. Your feelings about money are based on your perspective. This caused you to have a certain feeling or energy toward money. Whether your vibration is attractive or rejecting will become evident. So, understand that what you tell yourself about money is the same as what you might tell yourself about a situation or circumstance. It is absolutely critical to triggering the emotions that will come up as a result. Whether that be sorrow, anxiety and fear or joy, excitement and happiness is completely up to you and the story you tell yourself.

So how do you improve your emotional awareness where money is concerned? First you have to identify your current perspective about money. Then you identify how that story developed. Finally, you have an opportunity to shift the narrative and heal this relationship from the core by taking an opportunity to write your money story, if healing is required.

On the other hand, by increasing your consciousness, you will understand how to attract the abundance you truly desire.

#MINDFULMONEYMOMENT:
My Financial Feelings

How do you feel about money?

_____

_____

_____

Do you believe you have enough money?

_____

_____

_____

Describe a time when money triggered your emotional response?

_____

_____

| three |

Spiritual Awareness

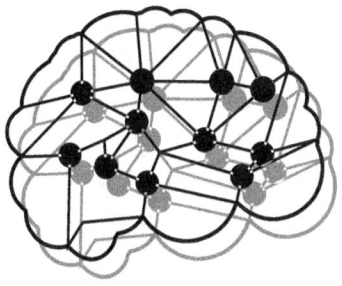

Pay Attention to Your Intuition

Your intuition is the sense of understanding that is instinctual rather than of a conscious nature. There are times when you just feel a sensation in your gut, in your heart, or in your mind that has nothing to do with your physical organs or functions. There is a thought with a feeling and a sense of fact about the matter. However, this feeling may come without any indication of logical explanation. Confirmation of intuition only comes with an experienced reality. While acting in harmony with our intuition demonstrates a level of faith, which means acting in correlation with the evidence of things yet to be seen. Second guessing this natural instinct, our sense of intuition, is a contradiction to our spiritual connection. Intuition is not about fear, it is about confidence. How well you pay attention to your spiritual connection, through your intuition, is an indication of your spiritual awareness.

Our spiritual awareness may be sharpened or dulled based upon our spiritual experiences. If you have experienced a nurturing spiritual environment where you are encouraged to explore and express your spiritual connection on an individual basis without judgment, even as part of a group, then you may flourish because of that encouragement. On the other hand, if you have experienced a judgmental spiritual environment where you are judged for expressing your individual spiritual connection, usually as part of a group, then you may have fallen subject to spiritual trauma or abuse and your spiritual connection will suffer as a result. To put it in simple terms let's make the comparison of our spiritual health to our physical health.

When you go to the doctor (like when you go to God or the Source) you are the only one able to speak about your physical experience from a firsthand perspective. When another person attempts to speak on your behalf you may receive a misdiagnosis or be mistreated because this person doesn't know what it feels like to experience life in your body. They don't know about the little aches and pains you may not have complained about to them. They don't understand the issues that have come up and gone away that may concern you as a matter requiring special attention for prevention or cure. This is the same as someone attempting to step in for you spiritually. They do not know your spiritual experience because they are not you. It's that simple. Their attempt to speak on your behalf or act in your place could cause damage leading to trauma and possibly turning into abuse. Let's keep in mind that the definition of abuse is when someone is treated in a less than caring and nurturing way. This also includes neglect, which can occur when you are not allowed to speak up for yourself as illustrated with the visit to the doctor's office. Does that make sense to you? Have you ever had this experience?

At times, people gravitate to spiritual groups in an attempt to meet their social needs. At other times, they gather with these groups in search of understanding and enlightenment. Oftentimes, unfortunately, they fall prey to judgment which leaves them vulnerable to influence against their own spiritual inclinations in search of acceptance. This is where the breakdown occurs, and spiritual awareness dissipates. A judgmental environment and/or culture will dull your spiritual awareness as you ignore your personal spiritual connection in yielding to a codependent spiritual connection. This spiritual codependency requires the guidance of others for a person to gain approval. This is not to be mistaken for true spiritual guidance in which another person teaches you how to make a spiritual connection and encourages you to continue connecting on your own, even as a member of a healthy spiritual group. In order to heighten your spiritual awareness, you must take an opportunity to be introspective and reflective without judgment. Recognizing your strengths and weaknesses honestly is a part of gaining a healthy spiritual awareness. Then taking an opportunity to discern the root of them both allows you` to lean into your strengths and improve your weaknesses with the opportunity to become spiritually stronger.

A heightened spiritual awareness lends us to an increased ability for discernment, which is a perception toward gaining spiritual guidance and understanding without judgment. Discernment is different from knowledge. You see, knowledge is what comes from study and research. Knowledge is about facts while intuition, discernment and thus spiritual awareness are about a connection to reality that is beyond cerebral processing. Allow me to reiterate that it's the feeling in your gut, in your heart, and in your mind that is undeniable and compelling without a physical explanation. Discernment comes from an internal sense of understanding that cannot be denied because of the Source from which it comes. Each of us has this sense within us. Each of us has this connection and our Mindset is directly affected by this Spiritual Awareness. In an illustrative way, it's about recognizing the Source that fills your cup. The Source is invisible and intangible, yet its existence is undeniable. Just like you feel the wind but cannot see it or touch it you are absolutely sure that it exists because of its effects. This is the same way the Source exists and the energy that moves does so without your permission. And it acts in harmony with environmental conditions which may be identified as the laws of nature. There are conditions that cause a cool breeze to blow gently on a hot day just the same as there are conditions that cause a tornado or hurricane to develop and grow, then dissipate after leaving a path of evidence regarding its presence and strength. My question for you is, what is the evidence that connects your reality to your dreams? Spiritual Awareness is all about recognizing the connection between your internal being and your external environment. This is where your imagination intersects with the creation of your reality.

In the next chapter the basic physical senses will be discussed, including sight, smell, sound, taste, and touch. These senses have also been mentioned in the previous chapter regarding Emotional Awareness. What's different in reference to Spiritual Awareness are the senses that are not necessarily connected to an identifiable physical function. Our senses of time, space, speed, intuition, peace of mind, etc., all fall into a realm of perception that we must acknowledge and understand to fully grasp our ability to manage our Mindset. Yes, I know about the vestibular system and proprioception, identified as the sixth sense, our sense of space, but go deep with me here. That reference is to our physical balance. What I'm talking about is our sense of space beyond our physical presence.

For those who have a heightened awareness of their intuitive nature, it's about honoring that inner voice of discernment and guidance. At times, it could be a warning of danger, a premonition about upcoming events. However, this sense of intuition and premonition is only confirmed with the reality that follows. A history of confirmations is what leads one to put a greater measure of trust or faith in the truth of what this sense leads us to imagine which becomes the reality that we experience.

By way of imagination there is the introduction to manifestation. Creating the reality of your dreams, or your nightmares, based on your perception and focus. Please understand that what you focus on in life is what you are sure to get, or experience, more abundantly. This is where the challenge of spiritual trauma or abuse can make a significant impact. Spiritual trauma can cause you to stop imagining or dreaming about the wonderful things that are the positive opportunity or the optimistic possibility in your own life. When there is an event or series of events that cause a person to question their core values and goals as the result of a toxic or damaging experience, spiritual trauma or abuse could be the underlying cause.

When a person begins to question their own values and the validity of their goals, it is often the result of damage due to toxic spiritual experiences leading them to an abusive perspective where spirituality is concerned. Remember, hurt people hurt people. When you have been exposed to a judgmental perspective as a familiar experience then that same toxic attitude may become incorporated into your own attitude and actions. When this happens the only way to heal is through a rewriting of your personal narrative. Spirituality is about love and respect for the Source and the resource, the Creator and the creation, the Universe and everything that exists in the universe. Your spiritual awareness is about understanding your role in the grand scheme of things and respecting the impact you have for both yourself and others.

This impact is based on the existence you choose to maintain with a spiritual connection or without.

When a person "does the work" to understand their Spiritual Awareness, then it may be consciously heightened allowing a clearer spiritual connection. This shift in mindset allows for greater intention. So now it's important to understand that Intention is the foundation of manifestation. Intention, however, differs from consciousness in that one may set an intention with their thoughts and subsequent actions without even being consciously aware of the laws they have set into motion with regard to action and reaction. This is when we find ourselves asking, "how did this happen?" or "why is this happening to me?" Our confusion comes about because the reality we created is not the one we'd prefer. However, through conscious attention to intention and focused manifestation we can cause a shift that changes the trajectory of our lives. Yes, we have that power. You have that power. It all comes through Spiritual Awareness.

We must respect the Source of all things as being different from the resource which may deliver the things we need. When we have an improper perspective and begin to look for salvation in other people then we have misplaced our faith. We must look inward for the spiritual connection that will truly lead us to the peace and abundance we desire and deserve.

At one point in my life, I learned to embrace scarcity because there seemed no other way. I spoke about the bare minimum as though not having enough was the expectation. I spoke about my great faith as though my having so little materially was a testament to the fact that God loved me. I was content with the fact that God was taking care of me and my family despite our limited resources and provisions. I was not taking care of myself and I was miserable and extremely uncomfortable. However, I was familiar with living this way for so long that my mindset had created an energy of contentment with the deficiency within and around me. It pained me at that time to see that there was not enough or to think that I had to accept the little I had and "make due" because in the depth of my spirit I wanted a better quality of life.

I've always believed that God has wanted the best and an abundance for me from day one. He is the creator of all things and those things are available to me as his creation. The thing I had to figure out was how to attain what I needed in addition to what I wanted while maintaining a strong relationship with my creator. The story of the three servants with the different measures of talents was a clear example for me.

So, that brings up our next question, how do you go about getting what you want? How do you create the reality of your dreams? To answer these questions there are two principles that stand out as undeniable in this process. First, that the success is in the setup and second, that the fortune is in the focus. Is your setup intentional? What are you focusing on? Setting intentions creates an energy, a tone, a foundation for building upon. Then very simply you will get more of what you focus on. So, where is your focus being directed? To what are you giving your energy? These questions are so significant because where you are at this very moment is based upon the answers to these questions for yourself personally within the past few years, months, weeks, days and moments.

Your intention and focus on the past, whether you were

conscious of them or not, is what's gotten you to where you are today. It would only benefit you to take a moment to contemplate and do a bit of introspection in consideration of these questions to determine how you got yourself to the station in life where you currently exist. Only after doing this work, of considering the past to the present, may you be able to now acknowledge where you are in life and then shift from the present to the future. That is where creating the reality of your dreams truly exists.

You may or may not agree with me about this next statement. I believe that everyone in life truly wants only three simple things: peace, love, and happiness, respectively. The way we each seek to attain them is what creates our varying life experiences and individual existence. There is a key to maintaining spiritual awareness. It is to keep in mind that no matter how important we may feel our own objectives are, there has to be something we respect that is bigger than self.

#MINDFULMONEYMOMENT:
My Money Vibe

What is my intention with money?

_____

_____

What do I believe about money in my community?

_____

_____

I am grateful for:

1. _____

2. _____

3. _____

| four |

Physical Awareness

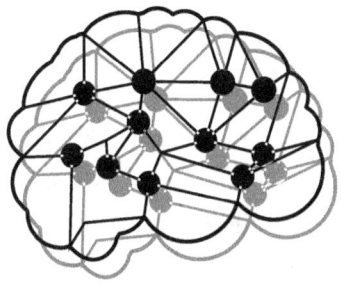

Pay Attention to Your Body

Now it's time to dig into those five senses, including: sight, sound, smell, taste, and touch. So here are a few questions for you. How conscious are you about how your body is functioning? Do you know the baseline healthy expectations? Are you familiar with what issues should be examined when they come up? Or are you just going along without regular maintenance checks? Are you acting like you have a junk car and you're just going to "ride until the wheels fall off"?

Your body is an amazing machine with the most incredible systems for operations, maintenance and preservation. However, your body is also subject to your treatment which makes all the difference. How well you care for your body will determine your longevity and agility. There is a difference between quantity of life and quality of life. My encouragement is to maximize them both.

Some people feel as though we are physical creatures with a spirit of consciousness while others feel that we are spiritual creatures having a physical experience. Whichever point of view you maintain, there's one thing that remains true. We all have physical bodies and an invisible spirit that work together to make us a whole person.

On the most basic level your body is a mix of organs, tissues and fluids. Some of those very vital fluids are your hormones. The release of certain happy hormones contribute to or "ADE" you in a positive perspective, including: adrenaline, dopamine, and endorphins. As a whole person you must remain conscious of how you care for your physical body in harmony with every other principle of mindset. I'm sharing this to help you understand how all of the principles of mindset awareness are truly connected and affect each other. Does that make sense to you?

There are senses within us such as our sense of hunger that reminds us to eat. Our sense of sleep guides us to get the rest we require to recover from our active lives. So, the question is what causes us to have these inclinations? How do we know what we need and why do we want what we want? Do you know yourself well enough to identify and understand the source of your instincts and inclinations? Having that knowledge is the result of understanding how spiritual consciousness is connected to physical awareness.

Your physical awareness by way of self-care is a direct reflection of your self-worth. The relationship you have with yourself is also of the utmost significance because how you treat yourself sets the standard for how you will allow others to treat you. Are you self-confident? How do you measure your personal value?

When you go to the doctors office you are the sole person responsible for the medical care you are given and the actions you take in harmony with any advice and/or prescriptions received. Yes, your doctor is accountable. However, they are not responsible for the actions you take. It's your body and you are the one who will receive all of the benefits or negative consequences based on the treatment you accept.

Have you ever been misdiagnosed and improperly medicated? No matter how much you trust medical professionals to care for you it is still your responsibility. If your doctors do not take enough of an interest in understanding the root of your health issues or prescribe treatments that you don't agree with, then you are able to seek another opinion. Ultimately the treatment you receive is dependent upon your consent.

I have learned this personally through some very tough medical experiences. Now I take full responsibility for any medical treatment I receive or refuse because I've learned in the years of healing and recovery that I must take the lead in my own health maintenance. I've embraced that I'm the only person who knows what's going on in my life 24 hours a day and who can have the most impact where a healthy existence is concerned. I've learned that many medical professionals tend to focus on the surface symptoms of an issue and often do not communicate with the other medical professionals caring for a single patient. When you have a primary care doctor, you might expect that doctor to be the one who coordinates your medical care but they are only responsible for managing the primary information within their scope of work. They're the doctor assigned to check your primary vital systems and refer you to the specialists when necessary or requested. They may ask you about follow up but having a medical conversation with a colleague about your health management is not their responsibility.

My encouragement is that while you continue to seek the guidance of medical professionals to maintain and improve your physical health, you might also be empowered to take the reins concerning the decisions that are made in that regard. Being a patient requires patience. There are no quick fixes. Healing is a process, on every level, and you must be willing to do the work in order to achieve viable results. It is very important that you understand what is required to accomplish your goal of becoming healed, healthy and whole.

Your physical experience is affected by your mental health, emotional well-being, and your financial status. It's so essential for each of us to pay close attention to what we put into and on our bodies, as well as, what we do with our body. Are you exercising, resting properly and eating well? Doing your body right means implementing a healthy routine to initiate and maintain your healthy body responses.

How you care for yourself determines how you show up in the world. How you show up determines the opportunities you can take and whether you will truly be able to benefit overall. So, take care of your physical health and continue to thrive throughout your life. Remember it's not just about how long you live but how well you live during that time.

#MINDFULMONEYMOMENT:
My Health is Wealth

What do I believe about my medical expenses?

_____

_____

What do I believe about the expense of healthy foods?

_____

_____

What do I believe about the expense of physical activities?
(i.e., sports or exercise)

_____

_____

How often do you do breathing exercises or meditation?

_____

| five |

Financial Awareness

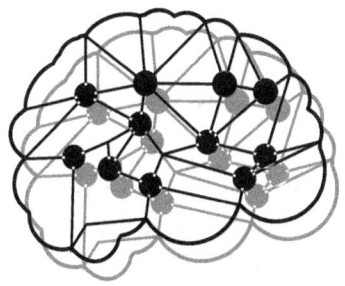

Pay Attention to Your Budget

There are only two things you can do with money; spend it or keep it. The basis then for financial awareness is a balanced budget. The balance is found when you spend enough to care for yourself in the present and when you keep enough to care for yourself in the future. When you understand the difference between how much money you earn and how much money you have as discretionary income then you will gain the perspective necessary to maintain a satisfying quality of life and be able to sustain yourself for a lifetime.

Once you have identified your necessary expenses then you can determine your discretionary income. Your discretionary income is critical because this is the money that allows you to do the things you want. There are ten major categories of spending to consider when balancing any personal budget. These categories include self-spending, housing, food, utilities, transportation, medical/health care, insurance, saving/investment/debt payment, entertainment, and miscellaneous. The first five categories are your living essentials, and the last five categories are discretionary. How much you spend on your living essentials determines your quality of life now while how much you spend with discretion determines your quality of life for the future.

For many people money management is a mystery. It can even be a very scary process when they don't understand how money works or how to make money work for them. I'm writing this book to break through that barrier and build a bridge to close the wealth gap that currently exists for so many in the world. It requires discipline and accountability. You can only accomplish the goal of taking your financial awareness to the next level with a healthy measure of determination and an unquestionable belief that starts with hope and ends with a positive balance sheet.

Many people have been taught that money is bad because of principal misinterpretations. Others have seen the detrimental results of greed. However, the use of a tool in a bad way has nothing to do with the intended purpose of that tool. In this way, money is not bad. Money is a tool that when used properly can be very productive. On the other hand, when used improperly money can be very destructive. Really, it's kind of like a hammer. You can use it to build a house, or you can use it to tear a house down. What's subjective is the intent and the skill of the one in possession of the tool. So just as with any other tool, the one with the greatest knowledge and appreciation for the purpose of the tool will respect it's power and handle it accordingly. What they choose to do with that tool is simply subject to their overall goals and objective.

As an actuator, money can only give power to the person managing it based on whatever character already exists within them. So, whether a person is generous or a person is greedy, having money only allows that character to show up; money doesn't create the character. It's not just about knowing that money isn't a bad thing though. The real issue for many people is understanding the traumas they have already experienced and how that is affecting their perspective where money was involved. The next phase of that is recognizing the impact that trauma could be having on their relationship with money from the past into the present.

You must pay attention to your beliefs about money. This is where you shift the narrative so that your "Belief System" carries you into action as you create the reality of your dreams. You must be conscious of the energy you feel toward money. Recognize that money has a vibration or a motion similar to that of ocean waves as the tide comes in and goes out. These are the waves of currency that come and go freely.

Be conscious of your financial cycles and operate in harmony with them. Be guided by your intuition along with a proper education. Take care of yourself well to elevate the value of your quality of life while increasing the quantity of your life. Be willing to take the time and do the work to manage your money and balance your accounts. So, a monthly financial review is absolutely essential.

Your reward is the result of your work. It doesn't have to be hard. Now is the time for you to learn and implement the strategies that will support you in working smart. In that effort, you must learn how money works and how to make your money work for you. Your management of money is directly affected by your care with regards to all five principles of awareness on this mindset side of the coin.

By taking a moment, or more, to do a bit of self-evaluation and introspection you will be able to identify your personal relationship with money. This involves understanding the five strategies for money management. In the second half of this book I will discuss them in detail as we dive deep. However, before you get there take a moment to go beyond the simple budget to create a balanced budget for yourself.

My encouragement is for you to choose a day in the last week of every month to schedule an hour or two for you to sit with your bank statements and your "Spend & Keep" Sheet* to track your actual spending for the previous month. Then take an opportunity to plan your projections for the next month using the Budget Balancing Sheet. Your "Time is Money" Tracker provides an opportunity for you to see where you're spending your time. As you know, where you spend your time is where you spend your money or where you make money through income producing activities. In the greatest sense, be a good steward to your money and it will be there to care for you and your family for generations to come.

#MINDFULMONEYMOMENT:
My Financial Routine

1. Schedule your monthly financial review. (Schedule the event on your calendar and set it for repeat every month on that same day or date, whichever works best for you.)

2. Print out copies of your planner forms from www.marimorlife.com/resources, including the "Time Is Money" Tracker, "Spend & Keep" Sheet, and the "Goal Setting" Sheets

3. Schedule your annual or quarterly financial review as a courtesy of your "Thriver" Membership Plan at www.marimorlife.com

How do you feel about creating your financial routine?

_____

How do you feel about keeping your financial routine?

_____

How do you feel about having an accountability coach?

_____

MINDSET RESET

Action Task: Breathe & Affirm

When you understand the physiological responses to emotion then you can manage emotional responses with thoughts. Here's a little something I learned about anxiety. When you feel afraid or anxious about something your body responds to the feeling by shutting down your normal physiological functions in response to the malfunction. This works kind of like the kill switch in an engine that gets over-heated. The overexcitement of the anxiety causes shortness of breath, dry mouth, pupil dilation and increased heart rate. It's as though your body is going into survival mode and shutting down all at the same time. It's truly a debilitating experience.

So, one day I was in the grocery store, and I was triggered. In the midst of one of these episodes I paused for a moment with the determination to regain control of my breathing and emotional stability because very simply, I didn't have time for a panic attack that day in the grocery store. {NOTE: Not to minimize the severity or impact of these episodes.} So, instead of feeding into the triggers, I paused for a moment and questioned the cause of this episode. When I realized that I had this overwhelming sense of scarcity I decided to tell myself the exact opposite to trick my brain into switching the physiological response from anxiety to peace. And amazingly enough, it worked! And it keeps working, not just for me but also for others. So, I know it can work for you too. Make the connection. Practice this Mindset Reset with breath and affirmation to overcome your trauma response and begin to thrive.

BREATHE: take two breaths in through your nose and exhale through your mouth.

This breathing technique is something I've learned to practice called a Hypothalamus Reset because breathing in this way triggers a release of your "happy hormones" contributing to an improved mood and state of mind. The reset may occur instantaneously. Taking multiple breaths in this way may also increase the beneficial effects. I'm not a brain specialist so feel free to do some research on neuroscience for yourself. This technique has been helpful for me and I hope it will help you too.

AFFIRM: repeat the MarimorLife Five Point Mantra as stated below

1. I Am Enough
2. I Have Enough
3. I Do Enough
4. The Source is My Provider
5. And So It Is

These five, simple statements are like the fingers on your hand. They make a complete thought and provide a strong, solid foundation to build upon when you bring them together. I am an Emotional Intelligence Practitioner, and this is my own creation. It comes from understanding the root of anxiety in personal experience. When I realized that my anxiety is created because of feelings of inadequacy and scarcity then I understood that it's necessary to shift the mindset by giving new energy to the thought process. I hope you benefit as much as I have from this simple but effective action task.

SIDE 2: MONEY MANAGEMENT

A coin only has value
when the one who spends it and
the one who accepts it respects it.

Now that you've done the work to establish your mind-set and increase your awareness, it's time to review the five principles of money management. This is where you discover what's in your best interest, literally. More often than not when people speak about money management budgeting is the first thing that comes to mind. While budget balancing is a significant aspect of money management it certainly is not the only factor.

On this side of the coin, I will discuss how you are able to contribute to your complete financial picture, like creating a financial portfolio or building a financial house as mentioned previously (See Financial Education). Those strategic principles include: cashflow, credit, savings, investment and insurance.

Consider that there are only two things you can do with money; the first is to save it and the second is to spend it. Hopefully you're doing them in that order so that you're able to track and control your money respectively. However, if you're not, the danger is that your money could "grow wings and fly away" when what you really want is to plant it like seeds in a garden so that it will grow like fruit bearing plants or perennials which yield additional growth and benefits year after year. In that case, understanding how to spend it wisely is of the utmost importance. So, now, let's review those five money management strategies.

| six |

Cashflow

Understand the Flow of Currency

There are many currencies in life. However, there are three which mainly contribute to the calculation of value in terms of cashflow including: time, energy and money. When you understand the exchange of currency then you will be able to manage your flow of currency. This means maintaining your financial power by managing your cashflow.

Let's review a few simple terms and definitions to support your strategy development. You'll need to understand these terms when you speak with your financial advisor. So, here we go.

Your cashflow in is your *income*. Your cashflow out is your *expense*. Managing a *positive cashflow* means that you have more income than expenses. Managing a *negative cashflow* means that you have more expenses than income. Having a positive balance is identified by the color black. While having a negative balance is identified by the color red. When your cashflow is at a negative, we call that bleeding. And yes, it's just that serious. So, when you hear about someone hemorrhaging money, you know it's pretty bad. My hope is that you never get to that point in your financial life. However, if emergency treatment is necessary be sure to reach your financial advisor for life support.

When you think about cashflow the main consideration is having enough income to pay for your essentials of daily living. That includes the first five categories listed on your budget balancing sheet. This can be found when you visit www.marimorlife.com/resources for a printable copy. The challenge comes in when your income is not enough to cover even those basic expenses. The solution is to find a source of income that is both legal and ethical to provide an increase of cashflow and meet your need. This is called making ends meet because the cashflow cycle is a circle. You start out with income and you want to be able to cover the expenses until the next flow of income. For most this cycle is calculated on a monthly basis. However, the cycle may be more or less frequent depending on your receipt of income and payment of expenses.

Another option for making ends meet is to find a way to lower those expenses. However, the lower you go in the cost/price for your expenses there will inevitably be an equal lowering in quality of life. The quality-of-life requirement is different from person to person although going below the baseline means living in poverty.

Please understand that I'm not judging anyone here. This is a no judgement zone. I've lived in impoverished conditions myself previously, so I know the struggle. However, knowing the numbers is where you'll find your power. Remember financial awareness. By being conscious of the numbers in your budget and projections you will be able to set goals. Goal setting can serve as a motivation for taking action. Taking the right action means producing the income you desire and require to make those ends meet. Have hope. If I could overcome those circumstances, you can too. That's why you're reading this book and taking advantage of every opportunity to elevate your financial situation. So let's get into the strategy.

Three ways to increase your opportunity for income are education, action and influence.

- Increasing your education means working smart so that you become a more valuable asset based on your knowledge and skill. You get paid for your contribution of intellect.

- Increasing your action means that you are getting a job done by labor thus increasing your renumeration. You get paid for the work you have accomplished.
- Increasing your influence means networking so that you add value through connecting resources. You get paid for your leadership.

The best way to increase your cashflow is to find something you enjoy doing and identify how to monetize. For example, one person desired to increase their income but was unable to spend the time working another job. The question was asked about identifying the thing that they loved to do most. They answered honestly that they enjoyed reading bedtime stories to their children. So then, the suggestion was made that they consider writing and publishing children's stories. Subsequently, they did just that and have found a measure of success doing that "work" which they love. It is amazing the opportunities that can be created when we think outside of the box in finding ways to increase our positive cashflow. This is just one example but there are hundreds and thousands, even hundreds of thousands of different ways to increase your income both actively and passively. The question I encourage you to ask yourself first is, "what is it that you most love to do?" The question here is really all about understanding your financial goals and creating a way to meet the income requirement either actively or passively.

Every individual must reach a point in life where they choose to take full responsibility for where they exist. Whether rich or poor, whether happy or sad, whether better or worse, no one else will do for you the things that you will do for yourself. No one else can accomplish your goals for you or give you the satisfaction that comes with that accomplishment. True freedom comes with knowing you have the power to decide for yourself concerning your income and your quality of life. That means taking on an entrepreneurial perspective, even as an employee. You must own your life and that means choosing what you will do for your earnings and how much you will earn in exchange for your intelligence, your time and your energy.

Have you reached the point in your life when you know that changes have to be made? Are you ready to get to the next level? Speaking personally, for a long time I gave away my financial power to another person. That period in my life was debilitating and stagnant. After many years though, I reached a point in my life in which I knew that I had to make some changes in order to increase my cashflow, so that I could accomplish the progress I required to establish financial stability. I also knew that I could only achieve true self-sufficiency with financial liberation. That meant a complete shift in understanding the role of money in my life and my role as the master of money in my life. For me, financial liberation meant reaching for more by going against the grain and stepping outside of the box I had placed myself in by granting another person the power to make financial decisions for me. That meant taking my financial power back by making my own decisions without requiring the permission of anyone else, aside from law and ethics.

As was described in Side One, I had to change my mindset and step up to a level of consciousness which required me to be aware of how much money I needed to earn in order to care for my needs. It started with that basic budget and expanded to a balanced budget along with budget projections. My greatest challenge was building that initial foundation on which to stand. Once I got started though, the snowball began to accumulate.

The smallest things can make the biggest difference. It's about how well you pay attention to your money that determines how much of it you're able to keep, protect and grow. Creating a cashflow strategy means determining the balance of the flow of currency based on your actual earnings and expenses while setting goals based on your desired future funding.

The most challenging part is truly not having enough when you don't know how to earn it or have not found the opportunity to work for it. Whether your situation or circumstances are described as poor, poverty or extreme poverty the simple explanation of that is just not having enough. This money management strategy begins with how much money you can make. Finding your gifts, talents and the things you love to do means finding the opportunities that will elevate you to a point of prosperity, abundance and wealth.

This starts with being able to see the opportunities that are right in front of you. I often refer to the illustration of buying a new car. For instance, when you go to the dealership lot to find a new car there are feelings of excitement, often combined with a bit of nervousness. However, you are looking to find something that is unique and meets the requirements of your preferences. So, you look around and find a car that's perfect for you. It's something that you haven't ever seen on the road before. So, let's say you drive off the lot with your new car. Amazingly, now you see three other cars just like yours on the way home. Well, it's not that they weren't there before you bought your car. It's just that now you've become more conscious of that particular style of car because it's the one you chose. The same scenario exists with opportunities. There may be the perfect opportunity for you right in front of you. However, if you're not aware of it or looking for the right features, then you won't even see it.

With this in mind, now is the perfect time to take an opportunity to review your goals and dreams. You'll want to identify how much income you require to accomplish them. The second challenge is figuring out how to make more money. Depending on your personal circumstances and the resources available to you, creating enough cashflow to care for your necessities and essentials may be more or less challenging. However, once you've completed your budgeting for present and projections for the future, then you may move forward with confidence, having the number in mind for what it will take to reach your goal. Now that you know how much you desire to earn as income, it's essential to examine how you will make that happen.

First identify your knowledge and skills. Second, decide if employment or entrepreneurship is better for you. Third, choose the product or service you will provide. The key here is to keep your eyes open for opportunities and be prepared to take advantage of the right opportunity that comes your way. A word of caution though is to be conscious of distractions disguised as opportunities. This can often cost you more in both time and effort without yielding any contribution toward your self-worth or your net worth.

The right opportunity will require you to make the effort and do the work to earn the return. Keep in mind that all work doesn't have to be hard, but it will require some effort on the front end for you to receive the residual on the back-end. The average person gets so caught up in thinking about how to pay bills every time they get paid that true cash flow never really becomes a factor for them. Their resources are consumed by debt and their lack of planning. When considering what new payments to take on they allow themselves to become subject to qualification rather than taking the responsibility to manage what is affordable based on their calculated ratio.

The solution is to create a financial plan or budget before you get the money you'll be responsible for managing. If you don't then that money will find a way to do its job without your direction. In that case, by the time you think to organize the money, it will be spent. This has proven to create a cycle of catching up rather than being ahead. So, make your plan. Stay ahead of the flow and create the reality of your dreams. Let's go!

#MINDFULMONEYMOMENT:
My Abundance Flow

What do I really love to do? How can I monetize?

_____

_____

What is the current amount of my discretionary income?

_____

_____

What is my personal breakeven point & income goal?

_____

_____

**I will accomplish my financial goals with a strong setup, a
firm focus and a die-hard determination.**

| seven |

Credit Strategy

Understand Credibility

There are two sides to every story. So, when we talk about credit then we have to have a conversation about debt. The strategy lies in how well you manage this twin power and leverage OPM (other people's money) to level up and accomplish your goals. This also requires understanding that there are two sides to qualifying for credit; there is personal credit and there is business credit. So let's chat about how this all applies to you.

In the beginning you are granted the benefit of the doubt and the privilege to manage money that doesn't belong to you. The question is whether or not you've been properly educated about the power you're about to wield. Do you understand the benefits and the dangers? It's like being given a flint and a match. You can start a fire to keep you warm or you can burn down the whole forest. How will you manage the tools in your possession?

Personally, I started the game without knowing the rules. I played improperly and had to pay the penalty for my lack of knowledge and poor financial decision making. I learned the hard way that credit alone is not an actual currency but rather it is a vehicle for managing your currency or cashflow. You'll read more about my experience in the upcoming Life Lessons volumes of this series. In the meantime, this is about understanding some basic principles and becoming familiar with the opportunities and options that are available in general. To truly understand how credit works you're going to have to do some research and schedule a consultation with a credit expert. (I'm not a credit expert but I make those referrals to my clients.) When you have your annual, semi-annual or quarterly financial review with your financial advisor, they will be able to look at your situation and circumstances to let you know what's in your best interest. That's where I come into the picture.

The most important thing about your credit is establishing and then maintaining a healthy credit profile. This is significant when you recognize that the numbers which identify your credit score are actually rating how good you are at keeping your financial promises. A credit conscious person is attentive to their score and understands how it changes. It's not overly intensive or stressful to be aware of what causes your score to increase or decrease, it's simply responsible. When your focal interest is about maintaining a high level of credibility then you will be conscientious about attaining a high credit score. You will also be more conscientious about the agreements you enter into and the way you extend yourself financially.

When a person understands credit strategy a few simple practices can make a world of difference in a short period of time. My credit recovery strategy was simple. I determined only to use my secured credit card for basic cash purchases that I knew I could pay off by or before the billing cycle ended. After doing that for just a few months my score jumped a couple hundred points to my surprise. Now I could smile about my credit score. Building up your credibility increases the opportunities and the privileges for which you become eligible. Keep in mind that if you pay off your credit card balance before the balance gets reported then a zero balance is reported, and it will look like you have not used the card. So, you can do two things to ensure that your usage gets reported each month: (1) contact the credit card company to find out when they report and (2) carry a small balance (between 2%-20%) into the next billing cycle.

When you use your credit card like you use cash and only spend what you have to pay back right away, then your credit card becomes a tool. But what if you have a mountain of debts and your income is underwhelming? That's when you need to consider your options for debt management and rethink your credit strategy.

Debt management is the process of caring for your promises that have not been kept. When things don't go the way you expected them to, whether your income changed, or you miscalculated the payback. This is when a restructuring is necessary to reestablish your credibility and overcome any negative records or ratings on your credit report. Remember this is all about reputation and credibility. The simple question is "How good are you at keeping your promise?"

#MINDFULMONEYMOMENT:
My Credibility

My credit score is: _____ My goal credit score is: _____

Increasing my credit score would allow me to:

_____

How much is the average interest rate on my credit cards?

_____

What is my current debt to income ratio?

_____

What is the **total** amount of debt I currently have?

_____

I am credible. I am incredible.
I am keeping my financial promises and creating a good
reputation for debt management.

| eight |

Savings Strategy

Understand Purpose & Protection

You've already heard this a couple of times so far. I'm just going to reiterate for the purposes of emphasis with this strategy. There are only two things you can do with money. You can either spend it or save it. Hopefully you save it first and then spend it consciously (according to your budget plan). By keeping track of your money, you are able to control it so that it will not grow wings and fly away. What you want is to have your money work for you. For that to happen you have to know where to put it so that it will be protected and have an opportunity to grow. This is where you pay attention to how you are funding your future; whether it's planning for retirement or saving for education expenses, holding funds for the purchase of your new home or establishing a capital base for funding your business.

Have you heard the saying that "it comes in like a dove and goes out like an eagle"? Well that old saying is talking about a paycheck that has been spent before it's even received. I lived for many years under that cycle of spending my money before I'd have a chance to save it. So, I know how it feels to put yourself in the position of not having enough from the start. The whole goal is to give your money an opportunity to multiply several times before it is spent. Once you get the concept and create the habit of saving before spending then your next step is to identify where you'll put your money for maximum growth and to minimize risk. That right there is about consistent, predictable interest growth over speculative, unpredictable returns. We'll discuss the speculative and unpredictable in the next chapter which covers investment strategy.

What really makes the greatest difference for successful savings is purpose and consistency. People save for a variety of reasons. Your specific reason for saving is only important to you. What matters most for the purpose of this conversation is simply that you have a purpose for saving. When you have a purpose for saving then you are more likely to pay attention to how quickly your savings will grow. Taking that into consideration may also encourage you to establish a more focused routine of saving. The key is to always do what will work out in your best interest. Paying less interest out and earning a greater interest on the money that you save or invest.

The most common way that people are encouraged to save is through the use of a bank savings account. However, there are a number of financial products that may serve as a holding place for your money. When you set an expectation, you will be a better tracker of your cashflow and keeper of the coins. Knowing that the average rate of interest earned from a basic bank savings account yields about .06% on the $1 and understanding what that means will help you to decide whether or not a 4% cash value account or a 10% investment account is the best place for you to put your money at the present time based on your means and your goals.

This simple chart will show you the difference:

My recommendation is that you find an account where you'll be able to earn a higher rate of interest while maintaining a lower rate of risk.

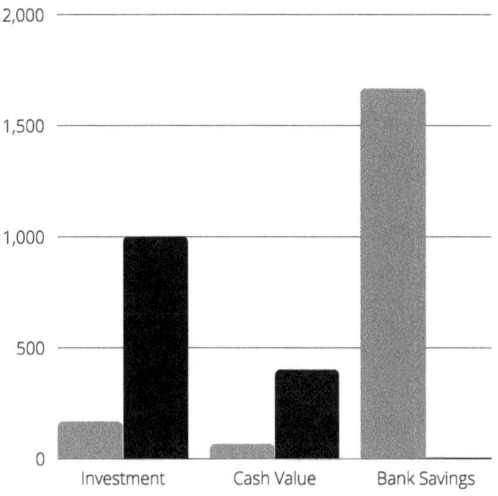

the amount of $$ it takes to earn $1 interest

estimated rate of interest for each account

#MINDFULMONEYMOMENT: Saving for My Life

What is my current purpose for saving?

_____

How much do I want to save?

_____

What is the interest earnings rate on my savings account?

_____

Is my savings protected from the risk of liens, fraud, garnishment,

and emergency? ___ YES ___ NO

My retirement savings goal is: _____

I plan to retire in ___ years with savings to last for ___ years.

I am preparing for my future with hope and confidence.

| nine |

Investment Strategy

Understand Growth

The scariest part of doing anything you've never done before is just getting started. It's like once you've done the thing it seems so simple. If you have to do it again it's nothing, right? Then if you have to show someone else, even if you've only done it once, you can sometimes act like a pro.

Yet, getting started can be like the monster you run from in the forest. You feel the fear without even knowing exactly what you're afraid of or running from.

Understanding how to get your money to work for you is the absolutely essential key to ensuring you don't end up working for your money for the rest of your life. That's why I do my best to create an experience which makes getting started simple and enjoyable. This is your opportunity to pay attention to long term growth so that you don't end up paying the opportunity cost for an opportunity lost.

For me getting started with investing was easy when I was young because I was offered my first shares of stock by an employer. They did all the work for me. They had the investment broker, they provided the stock shares, they even provided the payments and progress reports. All I had to do was say how much of my paycheck would go into the account each pay period. On the other hand, my experience later in life has been much different. I've been through a few things, my shares from that previous employer had been sold years ago during a time of hardship. So, any long-term growth I might have gained was the opportunity cost that I lost when I cashed in my stock.

Now though, I have reentered the investment scene without an employer account. It was a lot scarier than I remember. I mean, for the first time I was creating my own investment account. I set up a typical retirement account using an online service. I just answered a few questions, decided how much to contribute each month and clicked the start button. As simple as that sounds. I actually cried after clicking that button. It was like a release of the stress that had accumulated because of the fear I had overcome. In my mind it was the start of a new era for me. It was the breakthrough that I needed as I took the step to create something through which I would be solely responsible for my financial growth. The scary part though, was that I had to determine how much I would commit to paying consistently all on my own. There was no guaranteed that payment would come out of a regular paycheck because at this point in my life I had fully embraced entrepreneurship. This required a whole elevated level of consciousness and responsibility. It scared the @$!% out of me. When I set it up by clicking that start button to confirm my commitment I was like I'd opened the gates to a dam.

Yes, I cried, because of the uncertainty I had lived under for so long. I felt the strength of the universe was with me as I made this decision and executed my account. You want to talk about liberation. That was the defining moment for me. I was surprised at how emotional what a seemingly small thing could make me feel. I really didn't realize my fear was so deep until that moment. You see, I had set a deadline for myself that I wanted to have a stock account before my next birthday. In this event I was two whole months ahead of my goal. I just woke up one morning and I knew that day was the day that I would break what seemed like a poverty curse over my life. So, I did!

I share this story because I know that there are many other people out there who feel right now how I felt before I made the shift. Starting is not easy and starting over is harder but it can be done. It has been done. And for many of you, it has to be done. Whether you are starting or starting over, re-member to embrace the fact that you've had the courage and strength to make it this far in your own life. Take the next step knowing that you have the courage and the strength to make it through this too. You can and will accomplish every goal that you set for yourself, no matter how difficult it may seem. Just keep moving forward.

You've even considered investing because you have goals for financial earnings that go beyond what you can accomplish by exchanging your hours for dollars. Each individual must set their own goals. Then allow that goal to guide the investment objectives and portfolio strategy.

There are five major objectives for investing, which include: security, growth, income for lifestyle & legacy, tax minimization, and future planning. There are three main categories of investment that I encourage you to explore. They include Real Estate Investment, Securities Investment, and the Digital Market (crypto, NFT, Metaverse, etc.) As a financial advisor I have an extensive referral network. In that vein, if you're ready to take the next step on your journey to self-sufficiency then reach out. Join the community and get a free consult and referral to a financial specialist in the category that will best serve you.

Real Estate Investment is where you'll require the mentorship of a seasoned investor and the support of a great real estate agent. The key is to get properly educated before you spend or lose thousands of dollars, as I have.

I bought my first REI program back in 1998 right after I bought my first home. It was one of those Carlton Sheets programs that showed you how to find homes for sale by owner and turn a profit through flipping or residential rental. I had a sense of the right direction, but I just made a few wrong turns and got lost for a moment. Let's call it a 20-year detour. Now, that's a trip...LOL Anyway, the next REI for me came in 2020 when I invested in a system I felt would teach me everything I needed to know. However, I wasn't ready then either. Besides the COVID-19 Pandemic putting a pause on our global community I just didn't know enough to be confident about my next steps to create an opportunity to break even or make a profit with REI right away. Regardless of how many times you've made an effort to accomplish your goal or dream without success, just remember to NEVER GIVEN UP. Know that YOU WILL accomplish your goals and create the reality of your dreams.

And finally, I started studying and researching a bit about cryptocurrency and the block chain in early 2021. I've still got a long way to go there as well. Again, taking forward steps one at a time. However, I've got some really smart friends and I get to listen in on their conversations and even got to work on a plan for some major crypto progress. So if you want to chat about blockchain, call your girl and I will certainly direct you to my expert connects for that too.

Take that first step and keep stepping forward until you can say that it has been accomplished. Whether you're look-ing to create a lifestyle for yourself or generational wealth it CAN be done. Remember the hardest part is getting started and by reading this book, you've already done that. Congrat-ulations!!!

#MINDFULMONEYMOMENT:
My Best Interest

In what stocks do I currently invest?

_____

What type of real estate investment interests me the most?

_____

How much Bitcoin would I like to own?

_____

What other crypto currencies would I be watching?

_____

My financial advisor is: _____

My investment manager is: _____

I am worthy of receiving everything in my best interest.

| ten |

Insurance Strategy

Understand Risk

This is where you pay attention to how you are protecting your assets. When you spend money on something it is an investment. The thing is understanding whether or not you've made a good investment. A good investment yields a return. There are two types of return to be considered, including the emotional return and the financial return. A bad investment is one which yields a negative return or at the very least no return at all. So, when you contemplate making lasting investments you would want to have a plan in place to protect you against the loss of that investment. That's where insurance comes into the picture.

Insurance is a product which serves the purpose of mitigating the financial loss which is the risk when unforeseen accidents, tragedies and disasters occur. The whole objective is to protect your assets. Your greatest asset being the life you live, including the lifestyle you maintain for yourself and your loved ones. Thus life insurance enters the scene from stage left.

As a licensed life & health insurance agent I teach people about how to prevent the double tragedy that happens during the financial fallout after an emergency event has occurred. I've seen and even experienced the first hand affects of what happens when a person waits to apply for life insurance after having been diagnosed with a life shortening disease or in old age, close to their anticipated expiration. These are not always impossible times to gain coverage, but they are the more challenging times. Often ending with less coverage than is required or none at all because the client is unable to qualify for the benefits they need to make ends meet.

I've grown to understand that this waiting and procrastinating is often connected with money trauma that has been passed down through generations. The influence runs deep into the history of putting a price on a life. For some there is a great amount of anxiety connected to this concept. This because of the misconception that the only need for life insurance is money to care for burial expenses. An entire community has been held back from seeing and taking advantage of the true benefits that come from establishing a foundation of financial security through life insurance. Instead, there has been the mass trend of leaving behind the weight of debt that holds back necessary progress.

The benefit of a life insurance policy for many decades and generations has been highlighted in the lump sum received after the death of the insured person. The sad part is that I've heard people say that they aren't interested in making anyone wealthy because of their death. My question in response is whether or not they'd prefer to leave a weighted debt for their relatives to have to manage instead. No one wants their living to have been in vain. Furthermore no one wants to leave a negative memory because their family couldn't afford to honor them properly. However, over the past few decades the benefits of a life insurance policy have evolved into a greater **living benefit** than most people have been educated to recognize. Today life insurance policies are used for purposes that extend far beyond its original intention.

Understanding what life insurance really is and how it works are the keys to shifting from creating a legacy of wealth for someone else to establishing a quality of life for yourself that can exceed your initial expectations. When life insurance began it was for the purpose of keeping women and children from suffering destitution after the loss of a husband and father who was the sole provider for the family. Today women have the freedom to work and provide for themselves, along with any children they may have. Many women have taken advantage of the provisions available to even insure their own lives. They do this because they recognize the significance of the impact their death could have on the family. This is not just about the financial impact of their lost income but also about the emotional impact and how that will affect the family in terms of the time necessary for grieving and healing from this great loss.

I've found the greatest challenge for some of my clients, who are predominantly African American at this point, is the coming to terms with placing a monetary value on their lives. I've come to the conclusion that there are remnants of generational money trauma based on the fact that this concept was primarily introduced to our ancestors through chattel slavery. The racial wealth gap is real. While the reality of slavery no longer exists as it did, there are some very real residual effects to continue over coming. As an agent I see life insurance as a significant vehicle for rising above that financial challenge. Personally, I'm working toward a collective effort along with my colleagues to educate, guide, and support the black community in the US toward a more positive bottom line. We've been in the red for so long both by blood shed and financial deficit. Now its time for this community to truly be in the black as we recognize our value and create a reality that reflects that value appropriately.

For so long this community has been encouraged toward consumption and the temporary feeling of wealth that goes along with that. Now is the time to create a truly wealthy experience as reflected in the quality of life that is maintained. Regarding insurance, the community has been encouraged to supplement the foundation of the industry with temporary policies that do not contribute any significant returns. A term life policy certainly serves a great purpose. However, that purpose has nothing to do with financial protection with regard to quality of life or financial growth with regard to a legacy of wealth.

As you take an opportunity to review where insurance holds space in your financial portfolio consider the opportunities and options that exist for your wealth creation with your financial advisor. It is my understanding that insurance is the protection that provides a roof for your financial house. Be sure it's firmly in place, permanent NOT temporary. Be sure there's an opportunity for growth because that's where you get your money to work for you. You've worked so hard to earn what you have. You deserve all the benefits.

#MINDFULMONEYMOMENT: My Life & Legacy

For how much insurance can I currently qualify? $_____

How much money would I need to be able to live off of the interest?

_____

How much wealth would I like to pass on to the next generation?

_____

How do I feel about passing on wealth to my family?

_____

How much debt would I leave behind if I passed away today?

_____

I am creating wealth for future generations.

TRANSITION

Your Next Step...

You did it! You completed all ten steps. You now know the five principles of Mindset Awareness and the five principles of Money Management Strategy. Being able to identify these essential aspects for progressing on the journey to self-sufficiency will allow you to evaluate yourself, resolve any issues that you recognize and progress to the success you desire and deserve.

Consciousness is the first step in healing. Planning is the

first step toward creating the reality of your dreams. So I just have two questions for you:

(1) when did you decide to take your financial power back?

(2) did you realize then how much your mindset influenced your money management?

The hardest part about doing something new is getting started. So, I hope that reading this book and doing the worksheets has assisted you in overcoming that first hurdle. The next one won't be as tough.

For some people the challenge has been shifting from a poverty mindset because of not having enough. For others its learning not to live beyond the abundance of their means. Finding a healthy balance between spending and keeping your money is the whole goal. The objective is to fund your future and love your lifestyle. The ten steps you just read about provide a blueprint for you to create your own plan of action. When you clearly define your ultimate goal and identify the tasks necessary for you to complete the process, then you will be productive and continue making progress.

So, what's your next step? Create a Financial Plan and set your routine for regular Financial Reviews. Schedule an appointment with your Financial Advisor. (Visit www.marimorlife.com/services.) My recommendation from this point forward is to see your Financial Advisor like you see your Primary Care Physician, at least once a year. It is recommended that you see your physical doctor on an annual basis for a regular checkup of some routine vital signs for the purpose of maintaining and improving your overall health. The same purpose exists for seeing your financial advisor. With a minimum annual visit, you can have a review of all your vital financial reports and receive an analysis that will allow you to maintain and improve your financial health.

Just as when you see the physical doctor, a visit to your financial advisor may bring attention to an issue in your finances which requires a specialist to provide insight or support. Sometimes treatment and rehabilitation are required to get you back on a healthy track. Your financial advisor is the one who will diagnose your needs and make the proper referral. This is not the time to seek the advice of your loving family or friends who are not educated professionals in the field. Connecting with a professional is of the utmost importance for you to continue on the path to self-sufficiency and maintain successfully.

Now, that was the financial piece of it. Scheduling that appointment is something that you could continue to put off but why wait? Schedule it for at least a week from today and you'll give yourself enough time to do some Mindset work before you speak with your advisor. My encouragement, in the meantime, is to do the work of recognizing your own fears and the traumas that trigger them so that you may heal. You've heard the saying that hurt people hurt people. Well, I believe the contrary exists also, in that, healthy people heal people. However, I recognize from my own experience that there's also a lot of work involved. Time does not heal anything just because the clock is counting. In order to truly heal, a person has to be willing to do the work. Even when you have a physical wound or injury it has to be properly tended to and cared for, to heal well. What happened to you in the past doesn't have to define your future. Now is your time to thrive.

Whether you're just getting the hang of this adulting thing, facing a midlife transition, or reaching the stage of life that you once called "the future". Now is the best time for you to begin, review and adjust your financial goals. It's hard to know what healthy looks like when you've never seen it before. I do believe that our intuition or sixth sense, that sense of knowing that comes from within, can guide us when we're conscious enough to recognize the poor, unhealthy and detrimental habits and choices that must change in order to foster this new healthiness. There is so much truth to the statement that "health is wealth". As a person makes healthier choices on every level they begin to experience a wealthier lifestyle on every level also.

It's been proven that it takes approximately 21 days to change from one habit to create another. With that under-standing, we can conclude that there is only one way to improve this relationship you have with money and that's by changing your habits. So, I'm here to assist you in creating a routine that makes managing your money as simple as brush-ing your teeth. First, I'll be right here with you to show you how to get started and then I'll be here to help you keep up a regular routine. When we perform your financial check-ups and reviews you will be proud of your progress as you thrive in the direction you desire. It is a simple process and I'm here to serve you as your personal Financial Liberation Expert. I look forward to guiding you to self-sufficiency by teaching you about how your emotions affect your money management

Your first step is to connect with the MarimorLife Community at www.marimorlife.com/start. Once you've joined the community (at no charge), you'll gain access to special Community Resources and Community Rewards created and designed just to support you in taking the next steps on your journey to self-sufficiency.

It's time to get away from poor thinking and habits. Prosperity and abundance are realities that can become the truth of your experience in life. Pay close attention to your mindset. Stay aware, be conscious. This is the first step and the guiding step toward being healed, healthy, and whole. And finally pay attention to your dollars. It just makes sense to make cents. Know that the percentages are in your favor and make choices that are consistently in your best interest, on both sides of the coin. Continue with fortitude on your journey to self-sufficiency. Now is your #TYM2THRIVE! May you find and maintain peace and abundance without end.

Kevette Minor Kane is a financial liberation expert, an ambassador for "self-worth and gratitude" and a proponent for women's empowerment, especially for women in business. She guides her clients on their journey to self-sufficiency by educating them to take back their financial power and supporting them in gaining the confidence to fulfill their purpose in life.

Kevette understands money trauma and financial abuse because of her personal experience. She survived three major traumatic events in less than a two year period, including: surviving a major natural disaster and the devastation of the aftermath, the death of a parent and management of final affairs without proper funding, as well as, divorce after almost two decades of abuse. She has learned to thrive despite the challenges and obstacles many face in life. She serves because she understands the need and her passion is to ease or prevent the pain of others with her personal insight and wisdom from the lessons she has learned.

She has a Bachelor's Degree in Finance, is Certified in Emotional Intelligence and Financial Education Instruction. She is currently a candidate for both Trauma Informed Care Certification and becoming a Certified Financial Planner. She values continuing education and understands the correlation between emotions and money management. The goal is to encourage and empower every woman to establish and maintain a healthy and whole lifestyle. Kevette has done this work within herself and lives by the motto, "Never Underestimate Your Ability to Thrive."

As CEO & Founder of MarimorLife Mindset & Money Management her mission is to elevate women worldwide to a greater quality of life. She hosts seminars and workshops online. Kevette supports her clients through Financial Planning, Business Strategy and Mindset Coaching. As an educator, a public speaker and an author she shares her message of financial liberation through a transformational process which incorporates emotional-mental well-being with improved financial habits for continued success.

Kevette continues to serve her community to full capacity in her work through MarimorLife Mindset & Money Management. She enjoys connecting with individuals at various stages on their journey to self-sufficiency. You may connect with her as she provides a wealth of resources and rewards through the MarimorLife online community at www.marimorlife.com because she believes that now is your time to thrive.

Kevette Minor Kane, CFEI, CEIP
Financial Liberation Expert
MarimorLife LLC, Mindset & Money Management
Website: www.marimorlife.com
Social: @marimorlife (FB, IG, LI, TW, CH)

www.ingramcontent.com/pod-product-compliance
Lightning Source LLC
Chambersburg PA
CBHW060542130626
46553CB00002B/873